Rejoice!

GOD IS WITH US!

Rejoice!

GOD IS WITH US!

MARIE DOWLING, OCDS

LEONINE PUBLISHERS
PHOENIX, ARIZONA

ISBN-13: 978-1-942190-13-4

Library of Congress Control Number: 2015939136

Printed in the United States of America
10 9 8 7 6 5 4 3 2 1

Published by Leonine Publishers LLC
Phoenix, Arizona
USA

Visit us online at www.leoninepublishers.com
For more information: info@leoninepublishers.com

Dedication

This book is dedicated to all who
lovingly supported me with prayers and
encouragement, especially

my son Joe, and daughter-in-law Linda;

my daughter Julie, son-in-law Jonathan, and
granddaughter Sofia;

Discalced Carmelite OCDS Community
friends in Dallas, Texas;

and St. Bartholomew Catholic Church parish
friends in Fort Worth, Texas.

Contents

Foreword

The Presence of God is a theme very much in need of discussion in our society today. Whether one is Christian or not, this subject is echoed in many different ways in the lives of people of every nation and culture. Marie Dowling, who is a Secular member of the Discalced Carmelite Order, has given us a wonderful and creative reflection on the experience and meaning of the Indwelling Presence of God in her book, *Rejoice! God Is With Us!*

Rejoice! God Is With Us! is a book both personal and spiritual. The personal is founded on solid spiritual instruction, and the spiritual is enhanced by the original approach of the personal. Ms. Dowling offers Church teaching on how God is present to us, and provides opportunities to reflect on these teachings through everyday anecdotes and poetry of her own. Each chapter begins with a Scripture quote, which keeps the reader focused on the main idea of the chapter. Spaced between the chapters are poems, acting as meditations for the reader to assimilate the beauty and reality of the mystery of God's Presence in our lives. What I find most helpful, especially for a society caught up in the advancements of technology, is how the author balances the good of technology with the danger it can be in taking us away from God and distancing us from one another. Every day we are challenged by forces which want to separate us from God and thereby from one another. Ms. Dowling gives us an inspiring look on how we can develop a love of neighbor by cultivating a courageous and faithful love of God through the grace of His Presence. Young people particularly can benefit from this work of Ms. Dowling.

I have known and worked with Marie for several years. I am grateful that God gave her the grace to pursue this most important project amidst many trials; and I am grateful to Marie for opening this great mystery of our Faith to those who are seeking that deeper intimacy with Our Lord. God's presence in our hearts helps us to know His love for us, so that we can go and love one another.

God bless you all.

Rev. Jerome O. Earley, OCD
Mt. Carmel Center, Dallas, Texas
March, 2014

Preface

We have many communication tools in our highly technological world of the 21st century. Well connected with smart phones, computers, and the social media, we are always texting and e-mailing, which is not bad in itself. However, we need to have direct, personal communications with each other, not only with a "go between" gadget. To the Almighty God, the dignity of His creation is far superior to the materials we use today in our communications. Ignoring the personhood of others will eventually devalue it. Pope Francis recently said of the internet: "*This is something truly good, a gift from God.*" But he warned: "*The desire for digital connectivity can have the effect of isolating us from our neighbors, from those closest to us.*" He called for communications in the digital era "*to be like a balm which relieves pain and a fine wine which gladdens hearts…*" (Vatican sermon; January 22, 2014).

God resides in all His creation naturally, and is present as the Source of beauty, goodness and truth in all His creatures. Let us not avoid this Presence while indulging those things which may isolate us from each other; but rather let us look to find Him in our daily lives by doing what we were exhorted to do in the Epistle of St. Paul to the Philippians, 4:8:

> *...whatever is true, whatever is honorable, whatever is just, whatever is pure, whatever is lovely, whatever is gracious, if there is any excellence, if there is anything worthy of praise, think about these things.*

We are to *think of these things* and live in God's peace. Peace brings a certain tranquility of order in our lives. We seek this peace, so we place ourselves in a state of alertness like Elijah. We hope to receive what God wishes to give and we await His whisper with longing and patience.

This work would not have been possible but for the friends who supported my efforts with their prayers and wise counsel. I offer my gratitude to Father Jerome Earley, OCD, who was supportive of this work and gave input on its improvement. I also thank my Secular Carmelite Community, and my parish friends for their prayers and encouragement.

~ Marie Dowling, OCDS

"The just shall rejoice in the presence of God.
They shall exalt and dance for joy."
(Psalm 68)

INTRODUCTION

Rejoice! God Is With Us!

Do we believe in God, and realize His presence in our daily lives? As we go about our day, do we think of God and rejoice in Him? God still seeks us in this 21st century, just as much as we seek Him. However, many obstacles in our world keep us away from Him. We live in a world defined by technological advancements in communications, rapid growth in materialism and secularism. Integration of our Faith into our daily routines becomes more difficult when valued things interfere with the eternal value of people. The automated world leaves human beings out of the communication loop. Have you ever tried to resolve an issue by phone or online, and gotten nowhere because of computer programming? People don't help us today, and computers do not meet our needs.

Our society needs good communication tools for business and social networking; however, it can be too dependent on them, ignoring the role of persons in that communication. Our awareness of the presence of others may help or hinder how we seek the almighty Presence of

God in the world. Personal human to human communing is far better than machine to machine. We must not ignore the wondrous work of God: the human person. How many of us have observed a family texting at the dinner table, ignoring each other's presence? What about children who stare at a screen and ignore their brother, sister, or friend? Are we becoming so mesmerized by technology that we ignore the person?

Does ignoring human beings lead to ignoring God? This question has no definitive answer. Finding God's presence is paramount. We cannot see God, and yet we are commanded to love Him. So we respect the dignity of the person who is present to us and who needs to be loved as God loves him. In reality, we enter into each other's presence by the awareness of the other person. Being present entails seeing, hearing, feeling, knowing and attending to another's total humanity. Persons can sit next to each other, totally engrossed in texting or talking on the phone with someone else. Communing with another requires interactions well beyond the level of the senses. It requires a true encounter with the whole of our humanity: body, soul, and spirit (1 Thessalonians 5:23). This takes effort. Our selfishness makes us discount one another, and resort to the easier method of relating through a machine. The technological tool may become more important than the person. This mentality begins the devaluation of our personhood: that which makes us human.

God made us in His image and likeness. With that knowledge through our Faith, we enter into relationships with each other. We know that as God's children, we share that identity and long for communion with that likeness. We respond by valuing personal encounters such as family gatherings, and friends celebrating life. We love people, and seek fellowship with them. Nourished in these loving relationships, we grow to become whole: completely human. God looks at His creation and loves it. God loves us in our entire threefold totality of body, soul and spirit; in all that makes us who we truly are, made in His image. As baptized Christians, we can appreciate this likeness and live the mystery. We shouldn't dismiss from our life the similarities which make us human. Jesus came to bring our humanity to a sharing in His holiness. He is our *Way, Truth and Life.*[1]

> Sometimes the soul is distinguished from the spirit: St. Paul for instance prays that God may sanctify his people "wholly," with "spirit and soul and body" kept sound and blameless at the Lord's coming. The Church teaches that this distinction does not introduce a duality into the soul. "Spirit" signifies that from creation man is ordered to a supernatural end and that his soul can gratuitously be raised beyond all it deserves to communion with God (*Catechism of the Catholic Church,* 367, pp. 93-94).

The commandments and beatitudes tell us how to relate to God and other persons. We are commanded to love. Before we can do this, we have to be aware, be present, be cognizant, be in relationships, and then act. As people of faith, we seek God within our milieu. The quality of our encounters may reflect a measure of the degree of our faith in His presence. Why is this so? Charitable love warrants a personal involvement wrapped in a spiritual purpose: a purity of intention to serve God and give Him honor and glory. This personal activity brings with it compassionate caring, as depicted in the Gospel story of the Good Samaritan. The human touch still communicates charitable love to the other, and the action becomes holy when the intent is pure, originating from God's love.

Our search for God's presence in the 21st century becomes a challenge when we forget that we are pilgrims in a world bombarded by many distractions. God still seeks us in all of it. *"If today you hear his voice, harden not your hearts."*[2] Let us prepare to encounter the God who seeks us. This book has only one purpose—to invite us to an awareness of God's presence as we go through our daily lives. May He be praised forever! Amen!

"Your Face, Lord, do I seek."
(Psalm 27)

Chapter I

God, Where Are You?

Seven-year-old Mandy wanted solitude. The family gathering was so noisy that she left, and went outside on the porch for a while. The dark night was only lit by the moon and the stars. Looking up at the starry sky she whispered, "*God, where are you?*"

Immediately she felt overwhelmed with peace as if God had touched her saying, "*Here I am, my child.*" We know the truth of the innocent search, prompted by the beauty of nature and the delight of silence, and then that unmistakable blessing of peace.

Have you ever experienced an event in your life that made you realize God had a definite hand in it? Perhaps that event was so sublime and mysterious that you failed to acknowledge it, or to share it with others. Yet you knew that God's Hand was there. If you gained something positive from that experience which changed your life for the better, you are blessed to have received God's loving touch.

When we form ideas about the presence of God in our lives, we take from the Word of God, theologians and Church teachings. These ideas flow towards an understanding of God as Creator, Who generates movement within His creation as He rules powerfully over it. God gave each created thing or being an essence, meaning those natural characteristics which identify it. For instance, it is the essence of a seed to germinate, grow and become a flower, thereby producing its fruit. God's presence keeps this creation alive. So God is present by essence. God has no essence: God is... *I am who am...*[3] And this Being had no beginning and will have no end. God is eternal, infinite, almighty and all powerful. God is present by His own power. It is through the power of God that creation exists, is maintained and is ruled. Therefore, theologians write about God's presence by essence, power, grace, spiritual affection and substantial Presence in the Eucharist. Our faith in God is impacted by each of these.

"*Now faith is the substance of things hoped for, the evidence of things not seen.*"[4] There are two kinds of spiritual faith. One comes from the Church teachings about revealed truths, and the other is our own personal faith. In the history of the first Christian Church, the Catholic Church, the apostles and early Church fathers proclaimed what they had actually witnessed. Later writings of many were discerned and some chosen to be authentic books inspired by God, the Holy Scriptures. In the Creed, we profess these truths and we proclaim to the world our spiritual heritage. If we draw from the truths of the Scriptures and Church teachings, we draw closer to an awareness of the presence of God in our lives. God manifests His presence when a person seeks Him in faith.

It is appropriate here to discuss briefly the Trinitarian mystery. One God exists in three divine Persons:

the mystery of the Blessed Trinity. *"In the beginning was the Word, and the Word was with God, and the Word was God."*⁵ God the Creator made man in His own image and likeness; but man disobeyed, and in time the second Person, Jesus Christ the Word, became Man. He walked the earth, suffered, died, and arose on the third day. *"For God so loved the world that He gave His only begotten Son, that whoever believes in Him should not perish, but have eternal life."*⁶ The Holy Spirit descended upon the apostles on Pentecost Sunday to teach and guide the Holy Church. We believe in a Trinitarian God, and our whole perspective for growth in our faith journey is touched by this mystery. There are three persons in one God. We believe that our relationship with the Triune God is mediated through Jesus Christ; therefore, our relationship is with the incarnate God, Jesus Christ, whom we believe is both divine and human.

Through the ages, God has communicated with mankind through the writings of the Holy Scriptures. We may have a historical image of who God the Father is, who Jesus is, and who the Holy Spirit is. In other words, we create the images of who God is after reading the Scriptures. Knowing with our minds and not with our whole being, is different from encountering His presence in the Word. Within each of us the timing of our meetings in God's presence is a secret known only by the Almighty. It is by God's intervention, that these become a reality, a pure gift.

The presence of God by grace is within those persons who are not in grave sin, and are following His commandments. In some, a relationship starts with the Deity which is one of spiritual affection. This kind of presence is one described by the Discalced Carmelite Friar and Doctor of the Church, St. John of the Cross, in his Commentary on the Spiritual Canticle about stanza 11. He writes:

> *Reveal Your presence*
> *And may the vision of Your beauty be my death,*
> *For sickness of love*
> *Is not cured*
> *Except by Your very presence and image.*

St. John of the Cross explains three kinds of presence: by essence, grace and spiritual affection. There are *many kinds of spiritual presence;* all are hidden, since God cannot be revealed as He is. The three presences may be understood as the presence by essence, keeping all creation from dying; the presence by grace, whereby God abides in souls who are without grave sin; and presence by spiritual affection, which devout souls receive as He *"refreshes, delights and gladdens them."*[7]

As Catholic Christians we know the Presence of God in the Eucharist, and believe that Jesus gave us Himself in this beautiful sacrament. *"Whoever eats My Body and drinks My Blood has life eternal, and I will raise him on the last day...Whoever eats my Flesh and drinks my Blood remains in Me and I in him."*[8] This becomes our whole focus of public liturgical worship, the Mass, where Christ is present in His Word, in the priest, in the people and in the Eucharist. The Mass is the holiest act of public liturgical worship. Eucharist means thanksgiving, and all participate in thanking God, reliving the Paschal mystery and receiving the nourishment of the Word of God and the Eucharist. So there are five presences of God: by essence, power, grace, spiritual friendship and a real presence in the Eucharist.[9]

"*The awareness of God in our conscience is at the beginning and end of our spiritual life, and at the beginning and end of all religion*" (Moynihan, p. 1).

The awareness of God's presence does not happen in a vacuum. There is activity on both sides, for as God seeks us, we either freely move in His direction, or we move away. When we move closer, God draws us more deeply into a relationship with Him. What must we do to find this awareness? We know that in the revealed Word, Jesus states that we are to love God with all our heart, soul, mind and strength. Humanly speaking, we cannot love someone we do not know. Therefore, we reason that obedience to this commandment requires the capacity to commune with, to relate with, and to allow the other to enter our presence. Allowing the other to enter requires permission. God is a true gentleman, who gave mankind free will. Our own effort brings the readiness to receive freely, and God, Who always knows our hearts, comes when we are ready.

As we walk by faith, we begin as a child seeking solitude, asking questions such as, "Where do I come from?" and "Where am I going?" Seeking further, we find a value system which attempts to answer this type of question. But we are left empty, hungering for something more. We desire to know what is left out of our lives and we begin to seek the missing link. As we grow in wisdom and maturity, those questions are uncovered journeying through life with its trials and joys.

God is there for us when we need Him and we thank our parents or friends who introduced us to the sacramental life of the Church. Our initiation into the spiritual life was our Baptism when we became adopted children of God the Father, and as the water poured over our heads, we died with Christ and arose with Him. The triune God was present. That gift of grace made us His sheep to be pastured, whose names He knows and calls eternally. From that moment we were no longer alone. We started to grow in the knowledge of Jesus, who is eternal life. This sacrament of initiation opened for us other means of grace, especially in the Eucharist, His substantial Presence.

As baptized Christians we take the commandments very seriously and want to obey them. The first commandment to love God with all our heart, soul, mind and strength is there for us to obey, but do we know how to do this? We know we are to love our neighbor as ourselves, so we are charitable, promoting social projects to feed the poor at Christmas, or giving money during a disaster. But in our everyday lives, some of us do not appear to have an interest in loving God for His own sake. For "*religion as something relating to God, they neither know nor miss*" (Moynihan, p. 2).[10] We understand the humanitarian aspects of the faith, but fall short on the main reason we exist—to love God first. Vatican II brought that into focus in the writings about the mission of the Church. The apostolate of the people of God, the church, includes a sharing in her mission that "*the love of God and humanity is communicated and nourished.*"[11]

Perhaps we failed to learn, due to poor catechesis or the signs of the times which include materialism, secularism, and an indifference or irreverence for life from birth to death. Perhaps it is something in the human mind that rejects anything unseen as not there. If we don't see molecules does that mean they do not exist? We all believe there are things incomprehensible to our finite minds in the physical realm, yet we deny that there are spiritual beings, like God and the angels, because we do not see or hear them. We are not able to grasp the totality of the world around us, yet we do not acknowledge that a loving merciful God is the One generating it. By using human reason, we can know that God does exist by what is observed and what is known to be. The order and harmony of the world, the seasons, the multitude of planets, and the smallest of living organisms exist together with a purpose, as if to keep a balance and avoid disorder in the entire universe.

There are various ways to learn about the spiritual life, but the experiential way is most powerful. The early Christians heard the words of Jesus or the apostles and acted on them, like children obeying their father. We listen and discern in our world, asking what God is saying to us in our times. How do we react to that knowledge? We know God speaks through His Word, and through the Church. As the priest preaches and the word of God rests in our minds, does the word stay long enough to motivate us to act, or does it die soon after? These are questions which enable us to consider, and then respond to them. Learning requires not just the material presented to us by priests and teachers or by spiritual reading; it also involves our response to that stimuli, which in the realm of the spiritual life, could be life-changing. Let us say we hear the Word of God at church, and we do not act on it; instead we waste time that Sunday in recreational activities, and forget what the message was. We go about our week totally unaware of the message God intended for us to receive. We are setting our own priorities, and God's message is not as important as whatever we were doing after Sunday Mass. Responding to God requires faith, hope and love, and it includes a committed response to His Word.

In order to love God with all our heart, soul, mind and strength, we have to go through stages in our spiritual life, which include conversions, surrenders, self-denials and purifications. As we grow towards Christian maturity, we become more aware of God's infinite love for us, and gladly commit to the journey in faith on which He takes us. An experience of the awareness of God in our conscience and hearts helps us. This experience and inevitable surrender of our lives to God is an indication that we are learning how to love God. As we go forward with God's grace in our spiritual journey, that experience will remind us of the need for growth. Having a pure intention to please God becomes essential. When we maintain a holy life as His children, we remain in grace and God is present in us. If we fall from grace, we can be restored through sacramental means to our former state. As we grow in awareness of this holy presence, eventually we will share in the holiness of God, who alone is holy. When God gives us that gift, all three persons, Father, Son and Holy Spirit will come to dwell in us: "*If a man loves Me, he will keep My word, and My Father will love him, and We will come to him and make Our home with him.*"[12]

"*Lastly there is a presence of God not shared by all creatures, but limited to such of His spiritual creation, men and angels, as possess supernatural grace or its heavenly*

*fulfillment of glory: in these He is present by His indwelling,
for He really dwells within them as in His own temple or
home."*[13]

Just as seven-year-old Mandy left the family gathering and sought a quiet place to ask her question, we also
seek answers to our questions. God, in the quiet sanctu-
ary of our hearts, responds through the beauty of creation, the wisdom of the truth we seek, and through the
goodness of others. Readiness brings awareness at any
age. The essence of our encounter brings to fruition our
spiritual life, as we begin a relationship with God.

*"You will seek Me, and when you seek with your whole
heart, you will find Me"* (Jeremiah 29:13).

Today I felt embraced by the Lord,
Guiding me to yield to Him and cry
"Abba Father, come, take me to be yours eternally!"

How do I respond to this?
How do I conquer passion?
How do I love selflessly?

No other way but with a new heart
If God could take my broken heart
And redo it, only then
Would I begin to understand and
Accept the embrace, surrendering all to Him.

"I waited for the Lord and he stooped down
to me; he heard my cry."
(Psalm 40:2)

CHAPTER II
Waiting for God

Susan, a working mother, is driving home after a long day, thinking of how many times her family had to move to a different state, and how she may have put her will ahead of His. Praying with tears, she thinks of how the children had to be uprooted time and time again, and she asks God for forgiveness. Suddenly the radio goes silent, the wind is stilled, and a soft voice comes to her: "*But, I was always with you.*"

This mother, torn with grief over a family issue, was touched by God's presence in the ordinary event of driving home from work. When we learn to pray from our hearts, not just with our mouths and minds, we receive a response. As Susan prayed, the Almighty heard. He wanted to reassure her that He was present there, even in her doubts, even in her pain. Prayer is being truly present to God who loves us. Being present may be in a church, in the hospital, in the office at work, or anywhere our daily life takes us. Mental prayer is not a complicated matter: it is a decision to be aware of God wherever we may be, for He is everywhere and when we are in grace, God dwells within us.

Through prayer we are drawn to a relationship, to knowing and believing that God loves us and wants us to be present to Him and with Him. We learn about the teachings which prepare us for this faith encounter; then we proceed to an experience which God gently gives those who are ready to receive it. This may not happen as it did with the saints such as St. Paul or St. Teresa of Jesus. But, it will be an event which will touch us and change our hearts. It is through prayer that God blesses us with peace and love. This private moment may seem to be only for us; however, some saints like Edith Stein (St. Teresa Benedicta of the Cross) have written that all prayers of the baptized are communal, not private. We are united with Jesus and with all Catholics at prayer. "*Where two or more are gathered, there am I in their midst.*"[14]

Prayer is a means of growing in the divine relationship which supports us. We learn how we are to love the Lord, because while we are at prayer, the Holy Spirit teaches us. We embark upon the role of "disciple": the one being taught all we need to know. Through spiritual reading, especially the Holy Scriptures, we seek in meditation an application of the Word in our lives. As we seek, we find, and more is opened. "*Seek and you shall find: knock and it shall be opened to you.*"[15] We resolve to be actively mindful of God's presence in our lives the rest of the week. The awareness we find at church during public prayer continues as private personal prayer after we leave the structure of the church. We are to "*pray always*" as St. Paul reminds us in one of the epistles.

Our response to His presence furthers our relationship in prayer with God. This relationship can grow or be stifled. We can move forward in seeking God's presence, deepening our prayer life, or we can live in mediocrity. We decide. Just as we seek Him, He ultimately has been seeking us even before we were born. In the Holy Scriptures we learn how God knew us even before we were born. "*You knew me before I was born, in the secret of my mother's womb, you knew me. I praise you for I was wondrously made.*"[16] We need to remember how much we are known and loved! When we become aware of the depth of God's love we desire knowledge of Him and seek to please Him through acts of reverence, honor, gratitude, contrition, and supplication.

We demonstrate this gratitude by a life acknowledging and praising the God of our creation, our redemption and our sanctification. We worship Him in spirit and truth in our churches, in our homes and anywhere we are able, for God is everywhere. Once we become aware and form a habit of living in his presence, we develop into full Christian maturity. Brother Lawrence of the Resurrection, a 17th century Discalced Carmelite Brother, practiced the presence of God daily, and he received a growth in faith and the trust in God that gives true peace. His simple practice of living in the presence of God, even among the pots and pans, shows us the willingness of a humble person to commune with His God in all situations.[17] We can resolve today to form a habit of conversing with the holy presence we know exists in our hearts. We can resolve to be grateful for the Faith passed on to us by the Lord in His Church, and the personal faith He gives us as we live our daily lives.

A missionary priest shared these two experiences from his time in Africa. We shall call him Father Tom. Father had become accustomed to persons begging for food, but one day, a woman came with something hidden under a cloth. He wondered if she was going to ask him for money. She greeted him by name. "Father Tom," she began, "I am Sara, the woman you visited in the hospital years ago." She smiled and began to unwrap her bundle. She had brought six eggs as a gift for the kind priest. In that country in Africa, six eggs would feed a family for a day. This was a generous gift. Father Tom was very touched by Sara's gratitude to him. Years later, Father had to be hospitalized. One day, a young man came to see him and greeted him by name. "I am the son of Sara, and just wanted to know if you needed anything." Expressing thanks to good people is noble indeed. How much more should we thank Almighty God, whose eternal love for mankind was manifested by His sending His Son to save us.

Another time, Father Tom was entering a village, and saw an African woman ready to eat her daily meal. As she uncovered her small bowl of rice, she folded her hands in prayer, making the sign of the Cross and thanking the Lord for her meal. Both Susan and Sara displayed their faith in a prayerful relationship with God. One was touched while driving in her car. The other touched a priest's heart, for as Father Tom told the story, he was in tears.

Note: Narratives are true. Names, personal information, and settings have been changed to protect privacy and confidentiality.

FAITH IN GOD

Faith is Godly knowledge turned on fire.
It is the door to finding treasures.

Faith begins with firm convictions,
A stance and courage in the face of danger.

Faith envelopes the mind and heart to act
Towards God who is Spirit.

Faith compels and directs us toward the Light.
It energizes us toward goodness and love.

Faith is dark while we walk in life's journey.
It enables us to start and live a virtuous life.

Keep faith as your constant companion,
And live each day in God's presence.

"Be converted and accept the Gospel."
(Mark 1:15)

CHAPTER III

Following Christ

Pope Francis, after becoming pope, met with the media and mentioned the need to write about beauty, goodness and truth. Fr. Thomas Dubay wrote about these same existential terms that must be sought in the process of conversion. He quoted the six words Jesus spoke: "*Be converted, and accept the Gospel.*"[18] In those words we receive the mandate to change our lives and conform to the Gospel message. God does not want lukewarmness. God wants us to be holy as He is holy. We are all called to holiness.

Bishop Frederic Campbell stated in the recorded televised program "The Journey Home," that we all have three vocations. We have a vocation to life, to holiness, and to a state in life. We are called to be good stewards of what has been given to us in life. He acknowledged the work of the Vatican II fathers who wrote that we are all called to holiness. The Almighty alone is holy and we are called to participate in that holiness. We choose a state in life where we can best do the will of our Creator. He said that ninety percent of our mission is already laid out for us on the path to holiness, and the rest is our choice.[19] The idea of living out these three vocations makes sense, because our understanding of the meaning of our spiritual life begins, develops, grows, and matures. We are taught Christian truths as children, and they are modeled for us by parents, friends and those at church. As we grow up and enter adolescence and adulthood, we become more independent: free to discover for ourselves what these truths are and how to best live by them.

Our spiritual journey begins when we acknowledge these truths and begin to live a life in the presence of the Lord. If we settle for mediocrity in our spiritual life, we move away from the depth of God's love for us and what He has to offer us on our search for holiness. St. Paul states in one of the epistles that we run the race and do not look back until we reach our destination— everlasting life. To settle for mediocrity means we are not moving forward. We are stuck in a rut. We need to be determined to move forward, and this takes effort and grace. St. Teresa of Avila recognized the need to have a *determined determination,* when it comes to progress- ing in our spiritual life.[20] She taught her nuns to have this essential motivation to progress in their prayer life and in the performance of good works. She told them to move forward with humility, love and detachment, knowing ourselves and depending on God. We are God's creatures, His work in progress. We must obey His com- mands with hope, always acknowledging Him with grati- tude for every gift received.

Being converted, we seekers find what we hold to be good, true and beautiful, and also what may deter us from this search. As we seek what hinders us from living a life pleasing to God, we then work at eradicating those faults so we may go forward. This is not an easy task. We need a conversion of heart: a gift granted by God. While we struggle to eliminate mortal and venial sins in our lives, we eventually through grace reach our goal. We are able by grace to move forward. We start to be converted away from our selfishness and we exchange it for selflessness. As John the Baptist said, "*He must increase and I must decrease.*"[21] When we avoid sin and begin to grow in virtue, we more adequately sense our purpose in life. We make changes, some of them painful, and others pure joy. The desire to do God's will is now center stage. Discernment during this time might require an objective third person, such as a spiritual director or regular confessor. The Holy Spirit, who dwells in our hearts, guides our steps. We yield to God, as the poet stated, in a complete surrender to His will.

Conversion is a lifetime process because we tend to surrender to God gradually, as we gain wisdom from our prayer and practice of virtue. God continues to seek and guide us in our journey, and our ultimate goal becomes reaching eternal life, as St. Paul wrote. Slowly, we depend more and more on God, and less and less on ourselves. This is the opposite of what the world advocates. For the world tells us to seek and depend on ourselves and to strive for riches, fame, and pleasures. God promises us no real home here, for as pilgrims in this world, we are to have treasures in heaven where the moths do not get to them.[22]

We should seek only His will, His honor and glory, in the use of the gifts we have received. For example, if we have talents to teach, or serve the poor, we can act with a pure intention to please Him. Some will be unpopular

23

in the quests to witness to the Gospel. Jesus and His followers were also unpopular and persecuted. Some of us will be hated by the world, just as it hated Him. All of that will end, however, for Jesus told us not to fear, for He has already overcome the world.[23] He said that He will acknowledge before His heavenly Father those that acknowledge Him before men.[24]

Our God promises eternal life on high. Imagine, we will live for all eternity in dwelling places made just for us! So what exactly is this eternal life? *This is eternal life: to know God and Jesus Christ whom He sent.*[25] Therefore we are given this eternal life if we endeavor to know and love Jesus, the Christ, the One sent to be our Salvation, our Redeemer. We are not alone in this. Christ established His Church with a mission to evangelize and teach, with God-given power and authority. Jesus Christ, the source of all holiness, guides the Church in matters of faith and morals. Jesus nourishes us by His Word and the sacraments, especially the Holy Eucharist.

What does accepting the Gospel mean to us Christians after our conversion experience? It means a complete change in our hearts, in our entire lives. We now live to do the will of God, not our own will. We become docile and teachable, humbly awaiting His presence in our heart, His teaching through His Church, and His words as given to us by our priests.

Let us give an example of a conversion experience from Holy Scriptures. The Lord touched many lives while on earth; however, the apostles were the ones He most influenced because they were to be the evangelizers, and carry on His work. Their leader Saint Peter clearly went through several crises in converting to a man whose authority would be respected by the others. Peter was called and taught by Christ, and was given the leadership mandate. Peter denied Jesus three times, and then later was asked if he loved Jesus, for which he responded three times YES! The mandate to Peter was: *"Feed my sheep."*[26] Peter accepted what happened at one level, but it was not until Pentecost, after receiving the Holy Spirit, that he was able to boldly proclaim Jesus and the Gospel message. Peter went through three conversions in his spiritual journey: seeking God with his senses, then knowing and loving God in faith, and then acting upon what was being asked by the power of the Holy Spirit. Thus he remained in that unity of spirit until his death.

Knowing Jesus in our hearts by faith includes being open to our own conversion of heart. It means changing our attitudes, leading a life of grace, obeying the commandments, growing in virtues, seeking to perform acts of mercy and following obediently what God is asking of us. We begin to know Jesus who was sent by God. Our faith deepens. This faith taught to us by the Catholic Church now matures. By grace we grow to a deeper personal commitment to prayer, the sacramental life, and works of charity. When we surrender totally to Jesus Christ, our life becomes like a new creation, not because of what we do or say, but because of God's actions in us. It is as if God replaces that heart of stone for a real human heart. We now walk humbly with God, feeding the hungry, giving drink to the thirsty, loving our enemies and performing works of mercy out of love for Him.

Accepting the Gospel and acting upon it, means to hear the Word and then respond. We follow the call to love, not just our family and friends, but all those we encounter, and especially those in need of our help. Blessed Mother Teresa of Calcutta left her religious order to answer the call to care for the sick in the streets. She listened to God, who inspired her to be a witness of hope, and nurse those in need. She prayed with the hope of knowing what God wanted her to do. St. Teresa of Avila responded to that same call within her own monastery, and was driven to reform the Carmelite Order. St. Ignatius of Loyola was a soldier, who found through discernment that good reading material (the lives of the saints) gave him happiness which lasted; whereas stories of chivalry he often read did not. He wrote about his experience and became the founder of the Jesuit Order. There are other examples of holy people whose lives changed after an embrace of beauty, truth and goodness, for they were aware of His presence, and took a leap of faith. They hoped for God's will to be done and went forward in love to do it. What examples of virtue we have in our saints! They fully lived their humanity in union with God. We need to respond to this God who wants to lovingly transform us.

The best example of how to respond to God's call is Jesus Himself. For as the Son of God, Jesus constantly prayed to His heavenly Father, especially before a major event such as the selection of the twelve apostles. His mission began with a baptism and forty days in the desert, where he overcame temptations and resolved to do the Father's will in spite of the obstacles before Him. Our redemption brought Him enormous pain, and while hanging on the Cross, He thirsted for us. As God, He knew that even after dying for us, some would still not believe in Him. He arose from the dead, and was seen by hundreds who were blessed with His resurrected Presence. He ascended into heaven after giving the mandate to the apostles to go throughout the world baptizing in the name of the Father, and of the Son and of the Holy Spirit. Then God sent the Holy Spirit to live within the apostles and early Christian church members.

The early Christians had major persecutions to face. When they refused to deny their Faith, they were thrown to the lions. We think we have problems in our lifetime. Think of what they suffered, and what many still suffer in places that persecute Christians today in the 21st century. What about those who in the quiet of their hearts suffer what may be called a silent martyrdom, because of circumstances in their lives? Many are truly walking humbly with their God as *they live justly* and *love tenderly*.[27]

Knowing and understanding the historical accounts of Jesus in the Scriptures is one way to know Him. However, we truly encounter the biblical Christ when we learn to pray as Mary His mother prayed. How did she pray? Mary understood Her Son better than anyone, for she raised Him from a baby to adulthood. What mother does not know her child? Mary always listened to His words, and pondered them in her heart. She is the greatest saint of all! She obeyed God at the Incarnation, worshipped Him in her womb, and rejoiced in adoration of Him at His birth. Mary nursed Him, bathed Him, taught Him and lived daily with Him until His mission began. What lessons must she have learned just by being near Him! Mary understood God's presence, and as His mother knew and lived His pain as well as His joy. She asked Him to perform the first miracle at the wedding at

Cana, for there was no more wine. From the Cross, Jesus entrusted her to John the apostle and to the Church. The Catholic Church holds a venerable place for the Mother of Jesus, and from her example we learn how to pray within our hearts, in a hidden manner reflecting upon His Word.

We respond to the good news of the Gospels with faith, hope and love. For these, according to St. Paul in his letter to the Corinthians, are most important, especially love. In the epistle to the Colossians,[28] he reminded them about false teachers and how not to become captivated by them. He states that they have received Jesus, so now they should be rooted in Him, built up in the faith they have been given, and acting with gratitude for it. They are told not to be swayed by philosophies or teachings which are not according to Christ. There is much to ponder here, especially about this faith we have received. We Christians know that from the start, Christ selected a leader in Peter, who was to be the rock on which He built the Church. From this Church we receive guidance in order to continue to develop towards a clear knowledge of God with us today. We have a human and divine blending in the established Church. As the wisdom of our early leaders was manifested, it became clear that God intended to have Jesus Christ be the Head of the Church, with Peter as the leader on earth. God promised to protect His Church from destruction. This is indeed a mystery, because for over 2,000 years, we have had a succession of popes who are successors to Peter. Jesus stated that *the gates of hell will not prevail against it…*[29] And in spite of human failings prevalent in mankind, this Church continues today.

Our faith, hope and love are being tested in this 21st century, where secularism and materialism infiltrate our lives. We remain pilgrims in a world dominated by greed and the pursuit of pleasures. Yet we have only to look at Jesus crucified, and all the love portrayed in that act. That alone softens us; it reveals to us that life is about suffering for the other, about loving even when we are rejected, and of forgiveness when others are cruel to us. When we study the whole story of Christ, we need not seek any other love story, for none measures up to that wonderful story of our redemption. We are faithful followers of a God who loved us so much that He died for all mankind, even for unbelievers. We stand on sacred ground today because of that love which He gave us and keeps on giving us. That love is eternal; however, our response to this love of God leaves much to be desired. What will be our response when God calls us to convert and change our path?

The choice is ours—to ignore or to respond. Do we think we don't deserve this love, and therefore go backward instead of forward in our spiritual life? God wants us to respond to this call and not ignore Him. By pondering what we have been given, we can praise and thank God daily.

A woman once meditated in front of the tabernacle where the Body of Christ in the sacred species of the Blessed Sacrament reposed. As she prayed silently, a voice came to her in her spirit, "*People do not love me.*"

Immediately she asked, "Teach us Lord, how to love you!"

Loving Me means to open your hearts to My Spirit moment by moment daily. Loving Me means to

> *sacrifice yourselves daily, by renouncing sin, and renewing your spiritual life. Loving Me requires constant vigilance to know My will in your lives. Loving Me means to let Me inside yourselves, so I may change you. Loving Me takes courage and many never learn how much I want to be loved. Have courage to love Me today. Enter in and know how long I waited for you. You are all precious in My Eyes. I will teach you how. Do not be afraid. Come to Me. Love Me* (Anonymous).

We can increase our desire to be open and ready when the Divine Seeker communes with us. We can believe in His love, love Him above all, hope in the revealed Word which offers us knowledge of Him, and love in spite of our poverty and humble state. We can resolve to find the beauty, truth and goodness around us, and to commune within our hearts with this God who seeks us, the Source of all. The Holy Spirit guides us in any holy responses to the divine. The Spirit is there in our communal prayer at church where Christ is present. According to Vatican II, Jesus is present at Mass in His Word, in the celebrant, in the Eucharist and in the people. Jesus abides in the faithful, in the Word and in the sacraments, and from these we aspire to union with all God's people whether in heaven or on earth. When we attend Mass, we are being reunited with the Source of our existence. As we are mandated by the priest after Mass to go and live the gospels, we need to respond with a loud "Amen!"

After liturgical worship, we continue to respond to His Voice at prayer, by using our gifts and talents at work, and by loving our families, friends, enemies, and those in need. We move toward goodness and find in it a semblance of the Divine hidden within, for the Creator keeps all in existence. We have faith and believe in His presence. We shall not ignore the work of His Hands before our eyes. We can truly seek and find our God by keeping a close communion in personal prayer throughout the day. We need to find ways to tune in, to commune with the One who loves us. We like to use our phones to connect with those we love. Why not raise our thoughts in adoration to God whenever we are able? We do not ignore His holy presence in our lives. He answers our prayers, no matter how simple the request may be. Just as Brother Lawrence prayed among his humble duties as a Discalced Carmelite brother by having a conversation with God among the pots and pans, so we pray on the way home from work, or when we need help.

When we gain confidence in prayer, we act like the young mother Edith, on the road alone with her two toddlers. In spite of new tires, she has a blow-out, so she prays for help. She and her children go outside and wait. Soon a pickup truck stops, and three men of diverse ethnicities offer to help change the tire. They scarcely speak while they work, and after finishing their task, they disappear down the highway. You cannot convince Edith that those men were not angels, because in her mind, they were an answer to her prayer.

Nancy needs to finish a report regarding an accident she is covering for a newspaper. She does not know anything about the mechanics of a backhoe, or even what it looks like. Her report needs details, and the deadline is the next day, so she prays for help. Soon a male friend calls her, and proceeds to describe a backhoe in detail to her. In the middle of the explanation, a backhoe appears on her television screen! God listens, eager to fulfill our daily needs, even the small ones. For we know that God loves us; and answered prayer becomes a testimony of what He continues to do today.

Both Edith and Nancy prayed for God's intervention when they needed help. Without hesitating, they asked and God answered. No matter how small our concern, God wants us to call upon Him in prayer. By desiring God's intervention, we learn humility and hope in His love and mercy.

HOPE IN GOD

Hope is expectation for tomorrow's gifts.

It is the enduring longing for precious grace
Cascading down on converted hearts,
As they embrace their Light of life.

O Lord, You are the future all await,
The guiding Force of fortitude desired.

Keep us safely near Your Bosom, and
Bring us to the banquet of delight.

HOLY LOVE

Holy love, how wonderful your wisdom!

How incomprehensible your permanence,
In souls that know the Triune God and
Love the Deity in their activities of life.

Through holy encounters Love enters in,
Changing the focus, to see good in man.

Enabled by grace, your endearing face now
Discovered, accepted and seen in them.

Come, O holy Love, permeate our souls,
Blessing us in perfect tranquility.

"A new commandment I give to you, that you love one another; even as I have loved you."
(John 13:34)

Chapter IV

To Love as God Loves

Jesus said, *Where two or more are gathered in my name, there I am in their midst* (Matt 18:20). God sometimes answers prayers for healing, whether through the hands of a good surgeon, the sacraments, or intercessory prayer. An example will illustrate this. A Catholic woman we will call Marcia had left her home in the Midwest. She traveled to the southwest for colon cancer surgery. This was over thirty years ago. Her five sons had traveled from their homes to be with her at the hospital. While Marcia was in surgery, the five brothers were in the hospital waiting room on the eve of Pentecost, and they decided to attend Mass at a nearby church. They were impressed with the homily of the charismatic priest and asked him to accompany them to visit their mother and pray for her. Picture six men standing around Marcia, praying for her to be cured. God heard the prayers of the faithful sons, and the kind priest, and Marcia lived another twenty years. May God be praised for this example of love that the five brothers showed their mother, and for the kind priest who visited her. The three theological virtues, faith, hope and love, work together to enable us to love God and our neighbor. Faith brings us to believe and then speak, hope surrenders us to God's will, and *love bears all things, believes all things, hopes all things, and endures all things*.[30] Love is the most important, because as St. Paul wrote, it is the greatest of all and keeps all the others united. In the Holy Scriptures there are many passages which relate to this charitable love for others. Jesus showed compassion for those who were sick, possessed, left without hope, in need of mercy, hungry, lost or poor. Our hearts are touched after reading about the Good Samaritan,[31] the Good Shepherd,[32] the Prodigal Son,[33] and the Raising of Lazarus,[34] to mention a few. We can understand how tender and loving our Savior was when we read these Gospel stories. We've heard of loving others as we love ourselves; yet there is another love mentioned in St. John's Gospel: to love others as Jesus loves.

What does the new commandment mean, to love as Jesus loves? We read John's Gospel and see how Jesus acted with love for mankind. First of all, the disciples were directed to follow Him the whole way, from the Cross to glory. The love shown by Jesus was authentic and intense, even when facing the hatred of others. This love was one of humble service. He showed this love by how He lived and how He acted towards others. We note His words and actions and how He treated both unbelievers, and those who loved Him. "*This new commandment is the identity card of the true disciple. It is new because the measure of love required is the measure by which Jesus loves us, not how we love ourselves.*"[35] This love is like none other in its depth, beauty, truth and endurance. We are unable to comprehend it; yet in faith, we give to others what we have received—a peaceful love which surpasses understanding. "*No man has ever seen God; if we love one another, God abides in us, and His love is perfected in us.*"[36]

This command requires that we live by faith, hope and love, with a conversion of heart and a life of holiness. So to understand what this love actually is, we need to believe in Jesus Christ, keep His word proclaimed in the Gospels, and demonstrate this love in service to others. This love for our neighbor is beyond the love we may have for ourselves. Intellectually, we may understand it, but if we truly believed in it, our lives would change. Our perspective would be God's, not ours, as St. Paul states in one of his letters, "*to put on the mind of Christ.*"[37] For then the Jesus of the Gospels will instruct and guide us in the Holy Spirit. Our Heavenly Father would draw us to His Son in the Holy Spirit. The triune God will come and dwell in our hearts. This is what it means to be a real disciple following Jesus: to be alive with His grace in service, to use those first stirrings to love with compassion even those who hate us, to forgive those who harm us, to rejoice when we are tested, and to patiently await the peace that follows.

One of the most beautiful examples of love of the Holy Scriptures is that of the second-century writer and theologian, Origen. Benedict XVI, in his book *The Fathers,* wrote about his contributions to the Church. He explained the essence of praying over the Scriptures, an ancient prayer called Lectio Divina. From him, we received knowledge of this form of prayer which influenced St. Ambrose, the saint who baptized Augustine of Hippo. The great St. Augustine introduced this form of prayer to the western Church.[38]

When we read about Origen's love of the Word of God, and learn of the commentaries he developed in order to teach others about it, we know why he was able to develop the senses of the Word. He fell in love with the Jesus of the Holy Scriptures. Origen tells us that just as we have a body, soul and spirit, so does the Word of God. The body of the Word of God is the literal sense, how we historically know it. The soul of the Word is what we gain from it in our moral lives, how we understand it after applying it to ourselves. The Spirit of the Word of God comes to us passively, a complete gift from the Almighty: infused contemplation. St. John of the Cross, a Discalced Carmelite mystic and Doctor of the Church calls this passive prayer, obtaining God's *loving knowledge*.[39]

When we study and learn to pray with the Scriptures, especially the Gospels, we enter into a presence hidden within the Word of God. The Spirit within the Scriptures is received as a pure gift into our own spirit. In the process of praying over the Scriptures, there are four main steps which we follow. Each places emphasis on a part of the Word: body, soul or spirit. We can not only know the historical Christ as we read the Scriptures, but also go deeper, beyond the literal to the moral application of that Word in our daily lives. Praying about this and resting in the Spirit complete the process. So we read the passage, meditate on how it applies to our life, pray about it, and turn it over to God the Holy Spirit in contemplation. Reading, meditation, prayer, and contemplation are the basic steps in that process.[40]

The whole purpose of a life of prayer is to honor God and praise Him for all His gifts. Prayer is personal and communal, for as baptized Christians we pray in community, united in the Spirit received at our Baptism. Faith, hope and love are the theological virtues we have received, and our spiritual life is awakened when we live by them, especially love.

"Beloved, let us love one another; for love is of God, and he who loves is of God, and he who loves is born of God and knows God" (1 John 4:7).

"And behold I am with you always, until the end of the age" (Matt 28:20).

"We know that there are three comings of the Lord.... In His first coming, Our Lord came in our flesh and our weakness; in the middle coming He comes in spirit and in power; in the final coming He will be seen in glory and majesty."
(St. Bernard)

Chapter V

Three Comings of Christ

The Savior of the world first came to us in time: the Son of God, the promised Word of the Father, Emmanuel. We can ponder this mystery for a lifetime and never fully understand with our finite minds the totality of that event. Faith makes it possible to have brief moments of knowledge about this beloved Christ, born in Bethlehem. At Christmas time, we rejoice with the whole Church as we recall His birth. This is what St. Bernard called the first coming in history. Christ out of love for mankind took on flesh and weakness to enter time, to become one of us in order to save us. What a wonderful act of humility accomplished for no other reason but a great and holy love.

The second coming may be likened to our spiritual journey; we receive from Christ what He promised, for He will always be with us. In his sermon, St. Bernard stated: *"Because this coming lies between the other two, it is like a road on which we travel from the first coming to the last. In the first, Christ was our redemption; in the last, He will appear as our life; in this middle coming, He is our rest and consolation.*"[41] The road traveled is our spiritual life, whereupon we encounter Christ as being present to us. We develop on our journey in faith with our focus on the sacraments, and we grow in prayer as an effect of grace. St. Bernard quotes from John 14:23: "*If anyone loves Me, he will keep My word, and My Father will love him, and We will come to him.*" This middle coming or road traveled is how God loves us and seeks us throughout our lives.

Where does our personal faith journey begin? We know as Catholic Christians that the sacramental life of the Church provides us the resources to be nourished in grace. Therefore, the first sacrament of Baptism is our first encounter with Jesus, who came in time to save us and make us members of His Mystical Body as adopted sons and daughters of God His Father. From that encounter we received the necessary gifts to grow in the spiritual life. Some of us may have had other encounters within our personal walk seeking truth prior to our Baptism, like St. Paul's first encounter: hearing the voice of Jesus and being blinded by light. As we know, the next step for St. Paul was Baptism, which awakened him to new life and spurred him on to accomplish his mission. The importance of Baptism, where we obtain our faith, hope and love, cannot be overestimated.

We encounter Christ in all of the sacraments, which provide us with the graces needed to act in holiness. By our personal response, acting according to the principles learned, we develop a personal relationship with the triune God. Grace brings us closer to Jesus incarnate, and the Father, in the Holy Spirit, builds up a community of holy love in our hearts. This gift of sacramental grace becomes our personal encounter with the One who loves us, and guides us in this journey. We are never alone. It is through our encounters in the sacramental life of the Church and our personal life of prayer, that we grow to receive an awareness which transcends the knowledge about the historical Christ. Nourished by the Word of God and the Eucharist, our faith, hope and love deepen, and our awareness of Christ beyond the historical image ensues. We discover a Christ who satisfies our desires, the One who loves us, protects us, nourishes us, and guides us through our lives. "*Nothing can separate us from the love of God that is in Christ Jesus our Lord.*"[42]

For the sake of readers who may not know what the sacraments are and what they do for us, let us enumerate them briefly and explain how these became a part of our spiritual journey in faith. There are seven sacraments in our Catholic Church. What is a sacrament? A sacrament is an outward sign that gives God's grace. The first three initiation sacraments are Baptism, Confirmation and Holy Eucharist. Penance is the sacrament of reconciliation, which allows a person to be forgiven by Christ and seek a return to a life of grace with God. We are reminded of the prodigal son in the Bible and how merciful the father was. When we are living a life of grace and then sin, we need forgiveness and restoration, and this sacrament does that in our journey of faith. When we are struggling with venial sin, the acquirement of virtues, and other matters of morality, the sacrament of Penance is useful because the confessor could give us guidance.

Marriage and Holy Orders are sacraments related to our vocational call in life. Both sacraments are holy and prepare the person for a life of grace in Christ. The Anointing of the Sick is a sacrament of healing and may be received anytime we are very ill. For more information on the seven sacraments, refer to the *Catechism of the Catholic Church*.[43] The sacraments have a scriptural and traditional origin. The early Church Fathers and various holy ones throughout the ages report them as essential to our spiritual life.

Could the middle coming of Christ, described as the mysterious one, be compared to that generous love from God received at the conversion of the heart, which plunges us into another level of spiritual growth? When we convert and seek His presence, we begin to leave the mediocre life and seek a selfless life, a fuller receptivity for grace, and that knowledge of love and peace. That turning point experience presses us onward to a deeper devotion in living the sacramental life, to a frequent practice of prayer, to a performance of good works, and to growth in the virtues. We seek this coming just as He seeks our awareness of His presence during our entire lives: until we die and are no longer in time, but in eternity.

It is through the Church that Christ teaches us, guides us and nourishes us in our spiritual faith journey. In His wisdom, God provides us the means by which we can participate in His holiness. Out of pure love for us, Jesus Christ is present in the Eucharist to nourish us. If we did not need these means, God would not have originated them. Therefore, we need to be grateful to God for His wisdom and love for mankind. As this mysterious participation in holiness evolves, while nourished by the sacramental life and the Scriptures, the pure gift of loving knowledge or contemplative prayer comes. Love is received quietly and we become strengthened in our union with God. This union empowers us to perform good works and grow in the perfection of charity, or holiness.

This faith journey starts with our personal conversion and continues until our death. Baptism initiates this life in the spirit, and the growth of this life will depend on our readiness to receive it and God's plan for our salvation. Since the middle coming runs the span of our lifetime, it is like those stages of life: birth, development, maturity. The spiritual life as a journey starts with our Baptism and our acknowledgment of God in our lives. Each of us gives birth to this personal faith, and it grows to its final maturity of complete union with God. Those who are so blessed share in the holiness of the Almighty. They attain a high state of perfection in charity and we read about them as canonized saints.

This lifetime journey towards maturity as Catholic Christians generates in us an awareness of God's love for each one of us, and we respond with daily practices of good works. There may be a variety of comings as part of God's plan in the mystery of life. The Lord, the only holy One, guides us on this way of life if we cooperate with Him, as did holy persons throughout the history of Christianity. We see in the lives of the saints how a brief third coming could ensue, a profound knowledge in their hearts of a majestic and glorious Christ, while they still lived on earth. Through their own reports, written to teach about the splendors of the union with God, our saints declare how Christ entered their lives and completely transformed them. The spiritual experiences of St. Teresa of Avila give us an example of what these majestic occurrences may be like. Here St. Teresa writes about her experience of the continual vision of the Trinity:

> *The presence of the three Persons is so impossible to doubt that it seems one experiences what St. John says, that they will make their abode in the soul. God does this not only by grace but also by His presence, because He wants to give the experience of this presence.*[44]

The three comings of Christ: the historical, mysterious, and majestic, preached by St. Bernard can explain our prayer life. Praying with the Holy Scriptures brings us closer to the Christ who is the Word of God. At first we read and meditate about the historical Christ. The historical Christ is the One taught to us in the catechism classes or in Bible studies, and we acquire knowledge about him. We learn in the Old Testament how men and women of faith awaited his coming. For example, Simeon prayed to see the day of His coming and he did. As he held the baby Jesus in his arms, he explained to His Mother Mary that she would suffer much. As we learn about the Son of God Jesus Christ, we acquire a sense of what He was and is. But learning about a person in books does not take the place of meeting him face to face. Imagine a hero about whom you know a great deal, and whom you discuss with your friends. Then one day he comes to town. You would seek to meet him, to experience this encounter, to take pictures with your phone to show to your friends. Think how wonderful it would be to have this sense of who the hero actually is.

When we truly encounter Christ in our prayer life, the event is rooted in our hearts forever. This is not an image of what we were taught, not the historical Christ we studied in classes. This is totally different. The effects of this are these: we begin to pray deeply and to learn valuable lessons personal to us. The readiness to deepen our prayer life comes to us as a free gift when we cooperate with grace. Christ gives Himself to us in faith, and we begin to go forward, toward love, light and life. We begin to change. We care more about people, not ourselves, and we become seekers of the Source of truth, goodness and beauty within our surroundings. Others may take notice and wonder what happened. Some call this a conversion experience, others the reaching of another level or step towards God. But there are no words to truly explain a mystery. This is the effect of grace received. How the person got there is a mystery; but that person displayed effort or determination to grow away from selfishness to selflessness, and began a relationship with Christ, who is now an intimate Friend.

The relationship with Jesus begins with grace and our promise to renounce the world, the flesh and the evil one. If we were baptized as babies, our godparents made those promises for us, and as we grew and matured we understood this more and more, for we died and rose with Christ at our Baptism. Now we have experienced being an adopted child of the Father. What we are to become, how we are to journey, and what we are to accomplish in life by using the gifts provided to us is our choice. We grow in the three theological virtues of faith, hope and charity, which become imprinted in our souls at the initiation sacraments of Baptism and Confirmation. Now we are children of the Father, ready to be fed from the Word and regular reception of the sacraments. We rejoice because Christ is within us! Let us not forget the meaning of this experience, which deepens as we develop as Christians.

None of our encounters with Christ compares with the sacramental beginning, for grace is needed to be a follower of Jesus Christ. The Holy Spirit, the love between the Father and the Son, is present with the Father and the Son, when a person is in grace. We can only leave that state voluntarily by committing grave sin. God always listens when His children wish to return from sin to grace, and they are welcomed as the prodigal son was welcomed, with a robe, a ring and love. St. Paul taught us to keep the communication open with our God. The essence of any good relationship includes an intimate dialogue between the persons. Listening, speaking, and relating with God is the same, but in that prayerful relating, we acknowledge that our participation is one of reverence, humility and most of all: love. We enter into a dialogue with the Christ who taught us how to pray.

There are many beautiful definitions of what prayer is; however, the *Our Father* is one of the most beautiful, because it is communal, and touches every important area in our spiritual life. Jesus knew how important that prayer would become when we really understood its essence. Every petition in the prayer relates to our salvation, as Christ fulfills His mission of redemption and resurrection. As we grow up forgiving others, the Father honors our request to be fed daily, and so we are protected from evil until we reach the heavenly kingdom. Jesus fulfilled the promises contained in the Gospel

(Luke 1:71-79), that He would save us from our enemies and those who hate us, and that we would be guided into the way of peace. Jesus is the solution to all our needs!

As we travel this road, let us recall how Jesus prayed to His Father for all of us. This unity will enable us to grow into full maturity as Catholics, for without God's help we can do nothing.

"I do not pray for these only, but also for those who believe in Me through their word, that they may all be one; even as You, Father, are one in Me, and I in You, that they also may be one in Us, so that the world may believe that You have sent Me" (John 17:20-21).

"Let us make man in our image,
after our likeness."
(Genesis 1:26)

CHAPTER VI

Ignoring God's Work—Mankind

The 21st century may be different from biblical times; however, we still have the same hindrances to holiness: the world, the flesh and the devil. Through self-knowledge and God's grace, we learn how to deal successfully with them. As faithful Catholics, we cannot neglect the means available to us in the sacraments, and we resolve to follow the liturgical life of the church by attending Mass regularly, praying the Liturgy of the Hours, meditating on the readings of the day, and keeping away from the sources which lead us to sin.

People obey God when they find prayer to be a means of dealing with the hindrances to holiness. Jesus taught us that prayer is essential in this matter. He taught us this during His desert experience when He was tempted. Jesus taught us how to pray, how to be faithful in doing God's will in our lives, and how to act lovingly toward our neighbor.

Brother Lawrence has offered three suggestions: be pure in our lives; be faithful in our prayer life, practicing being in His presence in humility and love; and, to remember to mortify our senses.[45]

We may lack determination to accept God's call to change, and thus we do not progress in the spiritual life. But God is patient with us, and within our milieu He seeks us in spite of ourselves. Saint Thomas and other theologians believed that there are stages in the development of our life with God. They describe these three: purgation, illumination, and union, or, going from living in habitual sin, to conversion, and later entering union with the Trinity. However, our growth and development is not a sequential order, with a time clock ticking away as we reach one state or another. We are guided, and respond by grace to the presence of God, which transcends time. Faithful devout persons will be pure of heart, and only God knows their readiness for reception of gifts. Once we move forward in the spiritual life, we rejoice, for His presence will facilitate the rest of our journey in life. In simple terms this is a deep conversion to loving God, to pleasing Him with our lives, and praying deeply as we rest in His peace.

In our daily lives we have so many distractions, which may interfere with our seeking God in prayer, as we discussed in the Introduction. We live in a world which has become so automated that the very essence of our humanity is shoved aside. We gaze most often, not at people, but at a phone or computer. How can we teach our children that people are more important than gadgets?

The modern technologies increase to a remarkable extent the speed, quantity and accessibility of communication, but they above all do not favor that delicate exchange which takes place between mind and mind, between heart and heart, and which should characterize any communication at the service of solidarity and love (John Paul II).[46]

Here we have a holy man, Pope Saint John Paul II, writing about our communications. A *delicate exchange* does not take place with a phone, texting or emailing. It has to be a human connection, *between mind and mind*, between *heart and heart*.

Our obsession with technological objects may influence our young people's social growth. We may even lose the ability to problem solve, for we depend on the calculator to do it for us. A text, not even a phone call, may be substituted for enjoying a personal dialogue with a good friend. People need to use tools. But a misuse of these ignores person to person communication. God does not wish us to ignore the human person, nor cling to the objects created by man. We are not to ignore the work of His Hands. We should work towards having that communion in unity of mind and heart with those around us. Our relating has to rise above the material and technological tools. We are body, soul, and spirit, as St. Paul stated in one of his letters. The machines are just tools, people are real.

Relationships require relating in the true sense of the word: person to person; otherwise the relationship dies. When we use smart phones, laptops, email and texting, we do relate with our loved ones, but the person needs to be known in a deeper sense. If we loved our friends and never related to them personally at all, then we would question that love. But if we check on them regularly and see them often, we are expressing our care and love for them. In the spiritual life, the relationship dies if we don't find time for prayer; but God never leaves us. God waits patiently for us to love Him and to relate to Him in prayer. We have to find time to raise our minds to prayer daily, not by rote necessarily, but by truly conversing with Him about our current lives and what we are experiencing. We need to think of how to do this.

Blessed John Duns Scotus, a Franciscan priest, debated that Mary was born without original sin and won. In the movie of his life, there is a scene where a seminarian student apologizes to Duns Scotus for being critical of him in class. Knowing that this was a sign of unhappiness, John asked if he was happy in his vocation. Responding with an ambivalent answer, John proceeded to ask him what he first thought about when awakening. The seminarian stated that he thought of Mary, the girl who brought flowers to the church. Swiftly John explained to him what he needed to do to be happy in life and please God. So there is a scene where the student asks Mary to marry him. Reflecting on the wisdom of this Franciscan, we may note that who or what we love will be on our minds often, even at daybreak.[47] If we love God, we will think of Him at least at the start of each day, in the middle of the day, and at night. Our love for God eventually will become an ongoing prayer throughout the day.

"Seek first the Kingdom of God and all else will be given to you."[48] Our first vocation is to live life as a gift and seek the God who made us. Obedient to His commandments, we must have a prayerful relationship with Him and serve others for His sake. Dedication to the incarnate Word of God Jesus Christ, in a close relationship, is the

key to growing in the spiritual life. This primary relationship is nurtured in our lives by the sacramental life of the Church, by meditation on the Holy Scriptures, and by practicing the virtues. The deep prayer life which ensues becomes what St. Bernard calls the *rest and consolation*.

As we journey, we note the hindrances to growth in faith and in our prayer life. So we clear them away. One hindrance already mentioned is the misuse of technological communication. Pope Saint John Paul II states below how our words may ultimately acquit or condemn us:

> *Throughout the history of salvation, Christ presents Himself to us as the "communicator" of the Father: "God, in these last days, has spoken to us through His Son" (Heb 1:2). The eternal Word made flesh, in communicating Himself, always shows respect for those who listen, teaches understanding of their situation and needs, is moved to compassion for their suffering and to a resolute determination to say to them only what they need to hear without imposition or compromise, deceit or manipulation. Jesus teaches that communication is a moral act, "A good person brings forth good out of a store of goodness, but an evil person brings forth evil out of a store of evil. I tell you, on the Day of Judgment people will render an account for every careless word they speak. By your words you will be acquitted, and by your words you will be condemned."* [49]

In our daily work and even recreation, we can pray in a variety of ways, seeking the Divine presence and responding as we can. Maybe every hour we raise our minds to say a quick prayer, or maybe we find a quiet time during an office break. Some persons resolve to set a time to have a quiet lunch without co-workers, just to reflect on a Bible reading. Others walk outside to seek the beauty of nature and pray silently there. Some make a quick visit to pray in front of an altar in church if possible. Once resolved to do it, we can find a way. *"A word is the source of a deed; a thought, of every act."* [50]

Today technology makes it possible to click an app and read the Bible. We can choose to read about the lives of holy persons. Some did not always follow Christ. We learn about their human side, and see what changes brought about their conversions. In each life of a canonized saint, there are signs of the "why" and "how" they chose to follow Christ. Do we want to know their secrets? For example, in the life of a little known saint from Chile, St. Teresa of the Andes, a very young lady sought from confessors a formula for a life devoted to Jesus Christ. She made several retreats, prayed, and sacrificed to obtain discernment. She read the lives of two young saints: St. Therese of Lisieux and St. Elizabeth of the Trinity, who were Discalced Carmelite nuns. Both died very young, and are canonized saints. St. Teresa of the Andes chose to follow them as a Discalced Carmelite. She died of typhus at age 19, after spending only eleven months in the convent. She was allowed to take vows prior to her death. Pope Saint John Paul II canonized her in 1993, and her life has inspired many to grow joyfully in the love of God. [51]

Learning about our Faith, relative to its teachings and perspectives, also opens us up to growth in holiness. Those who seek Him are also praying. There are Catholic Bible studies, classes for converts to Catholicism, retreats, and workshops available in monasteries, online, or on CDs and DVDs. There are many tools to expand our knowledge base in the realm of dogma and truth. However, this is not enough. Our personal faith in God must grow too. This means that faith has to become real in our lives, personal in its expression, and selfless in its effects. We continue to commune with the Divine presence after Sunday Mass. If we do not continue, that personal faith will fade during the week, unless we are resolved to keep it alive.

As stated in the Introduction and earlier in this chapter, technology may help or hinder us in finding God's presence. Since these tools enhance our ability to reach out to the world, in the areas of education, media and social networking, we may think that its value is inherent, and that we cannot live without them. Recalling the words of Pope Saint John Paul II that emphasize our need for a human connection, we can resolve to act with our entire humanity, and not to misuse tools. God would not expect us to find in gadgets what is hidden in His human creatures. Our entire humanity has been redeemed and our entire humanity will need to be exercised in the work of salvation. When we reach out to the needy, when we evangelize, when we collaborate in science, art, cultural endeavors, when we solve problems, and when we give witness of our spirituality to the world, we respond with all our humanity. Our personhood is not to be ignored, for God created all of it. Let us praise Him for this gift!

An obsession with technological methods of communing may devalue life, change our culture and become a hindrance to our personal communication with each other, and ultimately even with God. Why is this so? We cannot ignore the work of His hands and expect to fulfill the mandates in the Gospel. Our personhood is a gift to others. We must fight the temptation to keep part of that gift and not manifest it in its totality. If we gave someone only half of a gift, the person would wonder about our sanity. What if we gave half a set of pajamas, or half a box of candies, or half a set of china? Gifts need to be given in their totality. In essence, we cheat others when we offer only an email for a thank you, or only a text to wish them well, and fail to meet them personally. These are ways to personally share more than just time texting them, or sending a quick email. We try to give our gift of time to the other in some personal manner out of respect for them. It is a lonely moment when we accept the gadget, instead of the person, as more important in our lives.

If we are truly Christians we look at persons as neighbors. Edith Stein stated:

> For the Christian there is no such thing as a "stranger." There is only the neighbor—the person who happens to be next to us, the person most in need of our help. Whether he is related to us or not, whether we like him or not, doesn't make any difference. Christ's love knows no boundaries, stops at no limits, doesn't turn away from ugliness and filth. It was for sinners he came, not for the righteous.[52]

We may miss that stranger if we misuse technological devices, because our focus will be on the gadget, not the person in need. We would be staring at a screen, not a human face.

With today's busy schedules, some families find it difficult to even have one meal together. At family meals children of all ages learn manners, courtesy, social skills, and a whole gamut of good helpful things, including how to share personally about their daily encounters. We acquire personal memories that we later treasure in our old age. How many of us can recall what we learned as a child while sharing a meal with our family? I can recall at an early age a great-aunt we can call Aunt Cecilia, who taught me how to use a fork properly. Aunt Cecilia told a story that has been shared many times at the table when children do not wish to taste a new food. She hated the color of carrots, and therefore did not taste them until she was fifty years old. Well, she found them to be delicious, and had spent all those years not enjoying them. So taste that new food first, we children learned, and then decide for yourself; and don't wait until you are fifty. Families need to relate to each other as human beings, and time away from the gadgets is essential to guard relationship building.

Relating to another person means to be truly present to that person. Then dialogue and sharing follow: essentials for any relationship to grow. How will we teach our children to value relationships more than a communication tool? Since our first social unit is the family, we need to hold the children to a time limit in their use of tech gadgets, especially at mealtime. Having a television in your child's room without any rules may not be an option. Children tend to overuse these and not get enough rest. Parents need to supervise the use of their child's television, computer, phone and other gadgets. We live our lives so connected to a wireless network that we sometimes fail to see the beauty, truth and goodness in our world at large. We may need a vacation from that wireless network.

All persons are made in the image and likeness of God. Can we truly find in others these qualities through the use of technological tools? What is missed in the dynamics when using these tools alone? People deny themselves the emotional, psychological, personal and spiritual qualities in the process of communicating. Let us observe our communications while using gadgets, and compare them to being truly present to those we love. Let us be alert to what makes for true relating, person to person, not gadget to gadget. Man is more than automatic responses. Man has a soul and a spirit; let us find methods which genuinely foster this type of relating with those we live with and love.

"For we are His workmanship, created in Christ Jesus for good works, which go prepared beforehand, that we should walk in them." [53]

"Late have I loved you, beauty so ancient and so new, late have I loved you! Lo, you were within, but I outside, seeking there for you..."
(St. Augustine, *Confessions,* Book X, 27)

CHAPTER VII

Love, a Pure Gift

The history of a love relationship which culminates in marriage is one of meeting, growing, loving and interacting. Finally there is a lifetime commitment. In the spiritual encounter with the Divine presence, there is also a type of history, a meeting and coming, a growing and prayerful interacting. Finally there is the moment when nothing else matters but to be with the Lord we love. Love demands that love be returned. Love seeks the other, wants closeness, self-expression and even intimacy. Love demands communion with the other, doing for the other, and even willingness to die for that person. True love demands nothing less than total dedication to the beloved, total self-giving, total transparency, total honesty, and a total gift to the other for life. One may say this is too much, but picture the love of a hero who gives up his life so that others may live, or a martyr who wishes to be true to his Faith and is killed because he cannot deny it. And there is that "silent martyr," the single parent, working two jobs to care for the children with a dedicated love and numerous acts of kindness. True love is a pure gift of self.

How does one learn love? We may think it comes from good parenting and good learning, and we may be right; but where did it all begin? Each of us was nurtured, loved, fed, bathed and supervised as a baby; and as we grew we looked upon our loving parents with some desire to be like them. We imitated how they walked, played and prayed. We acquired a sense of what life is about, what big persons do. We developed a sense of security and some idea about the good in people, which we realized was love. Goodness, one of the three existential, transcendental terms, was displayed in parenthood. Seeing others model goodness, imitating it, and later living it, brings us toward the sacred, the all Good, who is God. We learn to pray as we find the words modeled to us by adults.

As Catholic Christians we know that Jesus Christ as encountered in the Gospels is the most beautiful human being ever born. As God, Jesus is beauty, goodness and truth. No other religion but Christianity professes a Deity of beauty, goodness and truth, a God in three Persons, Who loves all men and died for all. When we learn about God, we respond with a grateful heart, a song of praise, a gracious bow, and a contrite longing. We humble ourselves before Him. "*A pure heart create in me, O God; put a steadfast spirit within me. Do not cast me away from your presence, nor deprive me of your Holy Spirit.*" [54]

"*God is love.*" [55] When we receive this Love and allow it to resonate in our hearts, we understand why we were born; and we embrace that purpose for our life. We were all born to give God praise, honor, and glory with our lives.

In our faith journey, we may begin by reason to see the universe in its magnitude and majesty. We may wonder what this majestic God must be like who created it. We may not yet have a loving relationship with God, nor have an inkling of how to develop it; however, we sense that in the created universe Someone is there much greater than we see. The connection between nature and God is a conduit towards a Presence, undefined at first, but much anticipated by the souls of those who gaze on it. As we behold it, we learn appreciation of its Source. As a child looking at the stars, we open our hearts to the love of God by gazing at nature's beauty.

All of us have a favorite person we admire for their goodness. It may be a parent, a mentor, a teacher, a saint; and we want to be like them. There are many who transmit goodness to others, and we note the selflessness in them, the fervor of their work, the prayerfulness of their lives. We wonder if we can possibly follow in their footsteps. We need grace to finally commit to changing our lives for the better. Grace brings us to our knees when we finally realize how much God really loves us. We have a challenge, great indeed. As humans, we want more direction, and we doubt our resolves. We need a moment of complete and utter conversion of heart.

We need a glance, an inspiration, a spark to initiate this loving relationship. We start with a dialogue, a prayer of desire, a sigh, a gaze at beauty, a cry while in pain, a need for solitude, a whisper of gratitude, and a longing for peace; but most of all, we start with a surrender of ourselves. Once we do this, we continue to do it every day thereafter. We need to implore this grace of Him who desires that we desire Him. He wants us to depend totally on His grace, His guidance and His love. We daily ask for mercy, for total surrender, for the light of wisdom to please Him in time with our minds, words and actions. This begins and continues our personal relationship with God. Our means of spiritual nourishment are given to us in Holy Scripture, in our sacramental life, in the Church; for we belong to God who made us and "*our hearts are restless until they rest in Him.*" [56]

Commitment to change to achieve growth takes plenty of resolve and determination. A conversion is needed to propel us forward, with grace and our efforts as God wills. Seeking and finding God's presence requires action from us, such as practice of the virtues, especially the theological ones of faith, hope and love. We resolve to be pure in our intentions to do God's will, to pray without ceasing, and to love as God loves. We fall many times but we pick ourselves up and try again. We start to change very gradually until one day we attain a sense of self-forgetfulness and look at ourselves, wondering how we got there. We continue to seek God in our world, and we pray daily for guidance not to offend Him. St. Teresa of Avila found that self-knowledge is most essential for progress in the spiritual life. Knowing ourselves keeps us aware of the most vulnerable situations.

We are bombarded with many distractions which enter our minds and affect us in accomplishing our faith resolves. Nonetheless, we can start each morning as a new beginning to devote our day to the Lord, and to offer up our sufferings, whether they are physical or spiritual, in union with Jesus for the sake of the Church. St. Paul says we should do this to make up for what is lacking in the Body of Christ which is the Church.[57] This ongoing devotion in the morning and at night, attending Mass regularly and using Holy Scriptures or the Liturgy of the Hours to meditate, will bear fruit. When we develop a habit of praying to the Lord daily, whether in formal prayer or informal communion, and we establish priorities for our days, practice of the virtues becomes good habits. This enables us to make progress in the spiritual life. We also begin to use our time more wisely and make decisions to help others in need within our community or in distant lands. We actively commune with God in that prayer which becomes active, a loving act, in our journey.

PRAYER: ACTIVE LOVE

Prayer is active love
Amidst the daily rhythm of life
Where presence of the Godhead Three,
Appears to captivate the mind.
Prayer uplifts the heart,
Provides food for holy growth,
It is as a force within the soul
That cries "Abba, Father, Come!"
Yes, come to heal our restless spirits.
Come, to soothe a painful longing;
To fill us with Your grace and to
Make us Your own again and again.
Prayer, as passive love, has no word or form.
It is grace on fire with desire for Eternal Truth.
It is communion which fortifies our inner self,
With wisdom, peace and love from our God.

"If you love Me, you will keep My word, and My Father will love you and We will come and make Our dwelling place with you."
(John 14:23)

Chapter VIII

Keep My Word

A beautiful four-year-old girl named Annie sits with her grandmother in the food court of a mall. Her mother has just left to order food and Grandmother is left in charge of Annie. But Grandmother is tired and unable to chase her. Just as Annie is about to run off, her grandmother asks her, "Do you love Grandma?"

"Yes!"

"Well, if you love me, do not leave me alone here. Stay until your mommy gets back."

The child becomes quiet, sits down and waits. Her love makes the difference.

God, in His wisdom, wants to protect His children from wandering away from Him. *"If you love Me, keep My word."* [58] What does that mean? It means to keep the entire truth that is contained in the Holy Scriptures, and that of the Church founded by Christ, Who remains as its Head. It was this Church which initially met to pray and break bread together, and later prayerfully selected these writings as the inspired word of God. The message of our salvation history has to be freely accepted, and lived in holiness by each baptized member, in union with Jesus Christ. This message is simple. God loves us, and we are to return that love to Him first; then radiate it to others by a life of service for His sake.

To love God with our all, to love our neighbor as ourselves, and to love as God loves: these are the very essence of our spiritual life. We may think, why make "love" a command? Just like Annie wanted to run away, but held herself back out of love for her grandmother, so we must not wander away from the truths revealed by God. We are protected when we live as God desires, and freely yield to His will in our lives. When Annie willingly listened to her grandmother, she changed her mind out of love. As we listen to the revealed truths and apply them to our lives, we begin in the direction of holiness. The message of Jesus becomes our mandate for a daily reflection, or an opportunity to help another. True seekers find the One sought in the daily routine of life.

When we seek and find the One, we follow Him as disciples, dying to ourselves, and living to do His will. We persevere in a prayerful relationship with Him daily. This strengthens us, not only to avoid hindrances, but to go forward, not committing faults of omission. Sometimes we lose opportunities to do good, mainly out of sloth or pride. We need to trust what God is asking of us.

Our preparing to be disciples warrants a desire to be last, and a desire to give of ourselves as a sacrifice. We follow a God who suffered and died out of love for us. Our love needs to deepen to include a denial of self for Him. That is why St. John of the Cross advocates that we mortify our appetites and journey to God in faith.

When love for another is godly, it is free and sacred, rich with blessing and pure in its effects. This kind of love is boundless, bearing much fruit. As imperfect creatures, we do His will only when He takes us by the right hand and leads us. We are never alone when we act in charity toward others, out of love for God, who is the source of all goodness.

We could obey God due to the fear of being damned. Or we may fear the loss of what we have now; the current state of things. The purest intention, however, is to obey out of love for Him. If we are undecided, and act in fear at the beginning, we can progress to a better intention later, as we mature. The connecting link here is our prayer life.

Through prayer we are building a loving relationship with God, who is pure Spirit. We enter into the deep prayer of mature Christians who are in union with God, like St. Teresa of Avila and St. John of the Cross.[59] As we grow in love of God, the Source of beauty, goodness and truth, we attain a relationship with God through His Son Jesus Christ, in the Holy Spirit. The Holy Spirit will guide us towards a life of selflessness, and we will be led to loving our neighbor as God loves us.

Our prayer grows with the death of our selfishness, a surrendering to His will, and the acceptance of our cross. A new beginning, gratitude of heart, and a sense of hope in His mercy, deepens our faith. We encounter life knowing that we are loved with a love that surpasses anything we could ever imagine! And so we rejoice, for God is with us!

"Go therefore and make disciples of all nations, baptizing them in the name of the Father, and of the Son, and of the Holy Spirit…and behold I am with you always, to the close of the age."
(Matt 28:19-20).

"Behold the dwelling of God is with men. He will dwell with them, and they shall be His people, and God Himself will be with them. He will wipe away every tear from their eyes, and death shall be no more, neither shall there be mourning nor crying nor pain anymore, for the former things have passed away."
(Revelation 21:3-4)

Conclusion

God seeks us daily. Our life journey is a mystery to us, but not to the One who made us. We wonder how everything in life seems to work according to some unknown schedule; and we go from day to day living and loving. Then one day, a crisis occurs and we react with a different perspective, not with panic as before, but with trust. Then we understand that this is not coming from us. We are now becoming totally dependent upon Him, and we see the changes and we marvel at God's mercy.

So we praise Him and look forward to another chapter in our lives, when every moment will be peaceful. So we walk in humility, by faith, and with the knowledge that in this world, there are hidden realities which are a matter of fact to the Deity who knows us.

Let us know, love and serve God, who first loved us. Let us return to Him all the reverence due Him, destroying all our idols, defending life, attending to each other as persons, and living in His holy presence. Amen.

Notes

1. John 14:6

2. Psalm 95:8

3. Exodus 3:14

4. Hebrews 11:1

5. John 1:1

6. John 3:16

7. *Collected Works of John of the Cross.* Spiritual Canticle, 448-449

8. John 6:55, 57

9. In the explanation of the five presences, the following authors' works were used to integrate them as a unit: St. John of the Cross, *Collected Works*; Fr. John Hardon, *Divine Attributes*; and Fr. Moynihan, *Presence of God.*

10. Moynihan, 2

11. Vatican II, Chapter 4, 51

12. John 14:23

13. Moynihan, 1

14. Commenting on Edith Stein, 158. Referenced in her biography by Herbstrith, and Matt 18:20.

15. Matt 7:7

16. Psalm 139

17. Brother Lawrence. *Practice of the Presence of God.* Brother spoke of the teaching of being recollected

daily, making it possible to understand and/or imagine God's presence at our work.

18. Mark 1:15

19. Bishop Frederic Campbell. Journey Home Interview CD

20. *Collected Works of St. Teresa of Avila: Way of Perfection*, 117

21. John 3:30

22. Matt 6:20

23. John 16:33

24. Matt 10:32

25. John 17:3

26. John 21:15

27. Micah 6:8

28. Col 2:6-8

29. Matt 16:18

30. 1 Cor 13:7

31. Good Samaritan: Luke 10:25-37

32. Good Shepherd: John 10:1-21

33. Prodigal Son: Luke 15:11-32

34. Raising of Lazarus: John 11:1-44

35. International Commentary 1487

36. 1 John 4:12

37. 1 Cor 2:16

38. Benedict XVI. *The Fathers*, 42

39. *Collected Works of St. John of the Cross*, 395

40. Fr. Morello. *Lectio Divina*, 19

41. St. Bernard's Sermon: God's Word will come to us, Volume: I Liturgy of the Hours, 168-9.

42. Romans 8:39

43. *Catechism of the Catholic Church*: Part 2, Section 1, Sacramental Economy, 280

44. *Collected works of St. Teresa of Avila*. Volume 1, Spiritual Testimonies, 438

45. Brother Lawrence. *Practice of the Presence of God*. St. Teresa taught that we pray as we are able, and Brother Lawrence made this practice paramount in his life.

46. Pope Saint John Paul II. Apostolic Letter

47. Blessed Duns Scotus movie

48. Matt 6:33

49. Apostolic Letter, Ibid

50. Sirach 37:16

51. Griffin. *The Joy of My Life: St. Teresa of the Andes*

52. *Edith Stein: A Biography*, 153

53. Ephesians 2:10

54. Psalm 51

55. 1 John 4:8

56. St. Augustine, Late Have I loved Thee

57. Col 1:24

58. John 14:23

59. Dubay. *Fire Within*, 13

Bibliography

Benedict XVI, Pope, *The Fathers*. Our Sunday Visitor Publishing Division, Hunington, Indiana. 2008.

Blessed Duns Scotus. Movie. Ignatius Press. 2012.

Brother Lawrence, *The Practice of the Presence of God with Spiritul Maxims.* Spire Books, Division of Baker Publishers, Grand Rapids, MI.

Campbell, Bishop Frederick, The Journey Home. Interview on CD recorded #JHC444. 10/10/11.

Catechism of the Catholic Church. Second Edition. Revised in accordance with the official Latin text promulgated by Pope John Paul II. United States Catholic Conference, Washington, D.C. 2000.

Dubay, Thomas, *Deep Conversion/Deep Prayer*. Ignatius Press, San Francisco. 1985.

Dubay, Thomas, *Fire Within*. Ignatius Press, San Francisco. 1989.

Garrigou-Lagrange, O.P., *The Three Conversions in the Spiritual Life*. Tan Books and Publishers Inc., Rockford, Illinois. 2002.

Griffin, Michael, OCD, *God, the Joy of My Life. A Biography of St. Teresa of Jesus of the Andes*. Teresian Charism Press, Hubertus, Wisconsin. 1995.

Herbstrith, Waltruad, *Edith Stein: A Biography*. Ignatius Press, San Francisco. Second English Edition. 1992.

John Paul II, Pope, Apostolic Letter. *Rapid Development of Technology in Media*. www.vatican.va/phome_en.htn. 1/24/05.

Morello, Sam Anthony, OCD, *Lectio Divina and the Practice of Teresian Prayer*. ICS Publications. 1995.

Moynihan, Anselm, O.P., *The Presence of God*. Revised edition. New Hope Publications, New Hope, Kentucky. 2002.

Newman, John Henry, *Life's Purpose. Wisdom from John Henry Newman*. Pauline Books and Media, Boston, MA. 2010.

Saint Augustine, *Late Have I Loved Thee: Selected Writings of St. Augustine on Love*. Editors: Thornton, John F. and Varenne, Susan. Vintage Spiritual Classics. Vintage Books, Division of Random House, Inc., New York. 2006.

Second Vatican Council, *Basic Sixteen Documents*. Costello Publishing Company, Northport, New York. 1996.

The Collected Works of St. John of the Cross. Translators: Kavanaugh, Kieren, OCD, and Rodrigues, Otilio, OCD. ICS Publications, Washington, D.C. 1979.

The Collected Works of St. Teresa of Avila. Volume I. Translators: Kavanaugh, Kieren, OCD, and Rodriguez, Otilo, OCD. IC Publications, Washington, D.C. Second Printing. 1987.

The Collected Works of St. Teresa of Avila. Volume II. Translators: Kavanaugh, Kieren, OCD, and Rodriguez, Otilo, OCD. ICD Publications, Washington, D.C. 1980.

The International Bible Commentary. A Catholic and Ecumenical Commentary for the 21st Century. Editor: William R. Farmer. The Liturgical Press, Collegeville, Minnesota. 1998.

The Liturgy of the Hours. Volume I. Catholic Book Publishing Co. 1975.

The New American Bible. St. Joseph Edition. Catholic Book Publishing Corp. New York. 1991.

The New Testament of Our Lord and Savior Jesus Christ and the Psalms. Revised Standard Version. Second Catholic Edition. Ignatius Press, San Francisco. 2002.

The Real Presence Association. Father John Hardon, S. J. Archives. www.therealpresence.org

Von Speyr, Adrienne. *The World of Prayer.* Ignatius Press. 1985.

Winifred, Nicole. *Pope Says Internet is a Gift from God.* Star Telegram Newspaper, Fort Worth, Texas. January 24, 2014.

About Leonine Publishers

Leonine Publishers LLC makes fine Catholic literature available to Catholics throughout the English-speaking world. Leonine Publishers offers an innovative "hybrid" approach to book publication that helps authors as well as readers. Please visit our web site at www.leoninepublishers.com to learn more about us. Browse our online bookstore to find more solid Catholic titles to uplift, challenge, and inspire.

Our patron and namesake is Pope Leo XIII, a prudent, yet uncompromising pope during the stormy years at the close of the 19th century. Please join us as we ask his intercession for our family of readers and authors.

Do you have a book inside you? Visit our web site today. Leonine Publishers accepts manuscripts from Catholic authors like you. If your book is selected for publication, you will have an active part in the production process. This book is an example of our growing selection of literature for the busy Catholic reader of the 21st century.

www.leoninepublishers.com

www.ingramcontent.com/pod-product-compliance
Lightning Source LLC
Chambersburg PA
CBHW021209020426
42331CB00003B/272